A BRIEF D

MW00638619

EIGHTEENTH CENTURY GAMES

M. Richard Tully

*A Brief Discourse on
Eighteenth Century Games*
M. Richard Tully

ISBN 1-893832-13-9

©2004 and 2006, Ballindalloch Press
Baraboo, Wisconsin 53913-1921

www.ballindalloch-press.com

❧ CONTENTS ❧

⇝ CARD GAMES ⇜

PLAYING CARDS have been around for centuries, and card playing was enjoyed by all social classes during the period of the American Revolution. According to Alexander Coffin, an American sailor who was captured by the British in 1781, even the prisoners aboard the infamous *Jersey* prison ship anchored near New York City were "playing at cards to pass away the time."

Note that in the 18th century, cards did not have index numbers in the margins (see the illustration on the opposite page). It has been said this was because most people were illiterate and could not read numbers, but anyone could just as easily learn to recognize the shape of an Arabic numeral as they could the unique pattern of pips on the face of the card. My own thought is that the card manufacturers felt that adding numbers to the cards was simply redundant and therefore unnecessary. Index numbers were first used in 1870.

WHIST

During the 18th-century, *Whist* was one of the most popular of all card games and is mentioned numerous times by James Boswell and other 18th-century diarists. It is a trick-taking game similar to modern Bridge and Euchre.

You will need a deck of 52 cards (no jokers) and four willing players. Card ranking is as follows: *Ace* (high), *King, Queen, Knave (Jack), Ten, Nine, Eight, Seven, Six, Five, Four, Three, Deuce* (low). The suits are all equal in rank—except the *trump* suit, which always ranks higher than any of its non-trump counterparts *viz*: the deuce of trumps outranks the ace of any non-trump suit.

The players cut the deck to determine the pairs of partners—the two high cuts play against the two low cuts. The lowest cut assumes the role of the dealer and deals out hands of 13 cards in clockwise rotation, one card at a time, to each of the four players. The *last card dealt*, which would fall to the dealer's hand, is instead dealt to the table and turned face-up for all to see. This card's suit becomes trump and it stays on the table until the dealer's turn (see below).

Partners sit opposite one another at the table and the player to the dealer's *left* leads the first trick by laying down any card he chooses. Each player then plays out a card from their own hand. Players *must follow the lead suit* (clubs, diamonds, hearts, spades) if they have it in their hand, otherwise they may play a trump card or "throw off" a non-trump card from another suit. The dealer may either play the trump card on the table, or pick it up and play a different card (note that the dealer *must follow suit* and pick up the trump card if he has a card matching the lead suit in his hand).

The highest card of the lead suit wins the *trick*—unless a trump card is played, in which case the highest trump card wins (see card rankings above). A non-trump, non-lead-suit card ranks as the lowest card played and can never take a trick.

The winner of the trick sets it aside and leads the next trick (the first partner to win a trick keeps his team's trick pile). The first *six tricks* are called the *book* and do not count toward the final score (sorry, that's the rules). Each trick taken after a team *makes book* counts as one point.

The winning partners of a hand may also score additional points during a hand. The Ace, King, Queen and Knave of trumps are called *honours*, and if the two winning partners hold *three* of these four cards, they score *two* additional points at the end of the hand. If they hold *all four* honours, then *four points* are added to their score.

In the 1700s the game point in Whist was *ten*, but in modern *English Whist* (known in America as "*Short Whist*"), the number of points needed to win the game is only *five*, and in modern *American Whist*, game point is *seven*.

CATCH-HONOURS

Scotsman James Boswell wrote of playing *Catch-Honours* (also called *Scotch Whist* or *Catch-the-Ten*) in the 1770s. This game is identical to regular Whist except that game point is *seven*, and when a trick is WON with the *ten of trumps*, it counts for *ten points* instead of the usual one point (a trick where the ten of trumps is played and then *out-trumped* by the Ace, King, Queen or Jack is scored as just one point). At the end of the hand, the *losing* team's tricks are subtracted from the *winning* team's tricks, with the *difference* being the winning team's score for that hand. So, even though game point is only seven, taking a trick with the ten of trumps might not automatically win the game!

SNIP, SNAP, SNOREM

This game can be played with almost any number of players and a full deck of standard playing cards is used. Each player should also have an equal number of chips or coins—all of equal value—to use as markers. The cards are dealt out until the deck is gone and if the deal doesn't come out exactly even it doesn't really matter if one player has a card or two more than another.

The *eldest* hand (the person to the dealer's *left*) puts any card in his hand down on the table, face up. Each player, progressing clockwise around the table in turn, tries to find the card in his hand to match what was laid down (*Three-to-Three* or *King-to-King* for example).

The first person to make the pair calls out "*snip!*" and lays his card down, making a pair. Play continues and the player who has the third matching card puts it down and calls out "*snap!*" The turn continues around until the fourth card is laid down to complete the set, that player calling out "*snorem!*" The winner of the trick picks it up and lays it beside him, then leads the next round by placing any card he chooses face up on the table as before.

Play continues in this fashion until someone plays all of his cards, at which point he collects markers from the other players—one marker for each card remaining in their hands!

The player holding the most counters at the end of the session wins! (The "official" rules don't really specify, but I imagine the cards would be collected and shuffled and a session would continue until each player has had a turn at dealing the cards).

Though the simplicity of play makes this game appear rather boring, there is quite a bit of strategy involved in how you play your cards! If you have two or three of a kind you will, of course, want to try to save them until someone else lays the remaining card(s). Also the shouting of "*snip, snap, snorem*" really adds to the excitement of the game, and the room can quickly get quite boisterous.

SNIP, SNAP, SNOREM—A VARIATION

An interesting variation on this game is described by Samuel Curwen, a merchant from Salem, Massachusetts. Curwen was a Loyalist and when the Revolution broke out he left his family and fled to London where he stayed from 1775-1784. Curwen attended numerous dinners and parties during his time in London, and in his journal he mentions playing several card games, but he does not describe any in as much detail as this version of Snip, Snap, Snorem.

Curwen states that in the game he learned, each player was dealt only six cards, which were played out as described above with the players trying to match up complete sets of four. (Curwen doesn't specify, but there would have to be a maximum of eight players in this version—it's probably best with only four).

By Curwen's description, the player who first matches the card that is laid down cries "snip," and the player who originally placed the card forfeits one of his markers to the pot. Likewise, when the third card is laid, the matching player calls "snap" and the player who had made the pair forks over TWO markers. If a fourth is played, "snorem" is called and the player who laid the third card lays down THREE markers.

Since all of the cards are not necessarily dealt out with this variation of play, matching full sets of four won't always be possible. Curwen doesn't specify, but if no additional matches can be made, it would stand to reason that the player who laid the last playable card (be it the *second, third* or *fourth* of the set) would lead the next round by laying down the card of his choice.

Play continues with the cards being collected, shuffled and redealt at the end of each round. The players continue playing and putting counters into the pot until all of the counters have been surrendered. The player holding that *last remaining counter* then takes the whole pot!

LAUGH AND LAY DOWN

This unusual little card game is mentioned in the diary of Thomas Turner, a merchant who lived in England just prior to the American Revolution. It is very easy to learn and makes for great family fun. It is for five players, and the general purpose of the game is to make pairs and *mournivals* (four-of-a-kind), by matching the cards held in your hand with cards that are dealt face up on the table.

You will need a full deck of standard playing cards and a collection of markers or tokens like coins, bits of corn, stones or (my personal favorite) candies. The tokens can be omitted if desired, but they do add a bit of excitement to the game.

Each player puts two markers into the pot, except the dealer, who stakes three. The dealer (chosen by cutting the deck—highest cut is the dealer) distributes eight cards to each of the five players, one card at a time. The remaining 12 cards are spread out on the table, face up. If perchance there are any mournivals among these cards the dealer picks them up and puts them next to him. If the dealer neglects to pick up a mournival, the first pl ve ⌐no spots it may take it up at the beginning of his t ⌐n.

Starting with the ⌐r to the left of the dealer (the *eldest hand*), players tak ⌐ pairing up the cards in their hands with the cards ⌐ table. Players pick up the matching card or ⌐ place the pairs or mournivals face-up next to t⌐ ⌐gresses clockwise from the dealer, and player⌐ ⌐ither *two* or *four* cards at a time and can ⌐y *down* one set per turn.

⌐face-up on the table, and you have the ⌐ pick up all three cards from the table to c⌐. ⌐nival.

The game s⌐ ⌐easy, and it is, but there are a few specific rules regarding turns and laying down cards:

• After the deal, if you have a *complete mournival* in your hand, you may immediately place it by you without it counting as a turn.

• If you have a *pair in your hand*, and someone else makes *the other pair* of that rank from the table, you may immediately place your pair by you without it counting as a turn since it can no longer be scored from the table.

• If you have a *pair royal* (three-of-a-kind) in your hand, and the *fourth* card is not in the pile, you may immediately lay a pair of it down since only one additional card is in play (so a mournival can not be made from the table).

Do these three things as soon as possible, or you may end up losing your mournival to another player!

When a player cannot make any more mates from the table, they must "lie down" by placing *all* of the remaining cards in their hand in the middle of the table for others to mate with. Only the pairs and mournivals each player has collected by them will count when scoring.

When only *one player is left* who has not laid down, the hand is over. The last player cannot make any more pairs, but immediately takes five extra markers out of the pot (for a total of six—see below). If any player did not take at least four pairs (eight cards) they must pay one stake into the pot for every pair they are short.

All remaining cards, both in players' hands and in the middle of the table, go to the dealer. Players then take *one marker* from the pot for *every pair of cards* over the number they started with. In other words, if a player ends up with only eight cards (the same as they were originally dealt), they take none. Ten cards earns one marker, twelve cards earns two, and so on. Since cards can only be captured in multiples of two, there should not be any "odd" cards left.

There are several strategies that can really add some excitement to the game of Laugh and Lay down.

First of all, if you catch someone else's mistake, you can benefit from it. For example, if the dealer overlooks a mournival on the table, the person who notices it first can take it (the dealer should be given ample time to notice the mournival). Likewise, if a *pair royal* (three-of-a-kind) is on the table, and a player takes only one away, the player who notices can take the remaining pair.

Also, if you have a pair royal in your hand, and only lay down a pair of it by you, someone who notices it at the end of the game (when your cards are laid down) can *take your remaining card* to make a pair for themselves.

Of course, the object of the game is to stay in play for as long as possible. Here are a few pointers to help you along:

• If you have a pair royal in your hand, and the fourth card is on the table, leave it for last—no one else can take it (just don't forget)!

• If you have a pair in your hand, and the corresponding pair is on the table, leave it for later as no one else can claim it.

• If a pair is on the table, and you have a third, you are guaranteed one of the pair on the table (only matching cards that complete a set of twos or fours can be picked up, so if one card is picked up for a pair you are the only player who can pick up the last card), so leave it for later.

• If you have a single card in your hand that matches a single card on the table—take it as soon as possible!

QUINZE

This game comes from the 1779 edition of *Hoyle's Games Improved*. Quinze is almost identical to our modern game of *Twenty-one*, or *Blackjack*, with the primary difference being that game point is only 15, hence the name *Quinze* (the French word for the number 15). It is normally played by just two players, but more can play as well.

The cards are all rated at their face value, (the *Ace* is worth one, the *Deuce* is worth two, the *Trois* is worth three, *&c.*) but all court cards, i.e. the *Kings*, *Queens* and *Jacks*, are worth ten points each. Hence, 16 of the cards in a pack of 52 are valued at ten points, so the chances of drawing a ten are about three-to-one.

The cards are cut by each player, and the highest card deals. The cards are shuffled, and the adversary cuts them. The dealer now deals one card to his adversary and one to himself, both face down. The players may now look at their card and take turns requesting one or more additional cards from the dealer. The object is to come as close to 15 as possible without going over.

Note that there are no "naturals" in Quinze, for it is impossible to score 15 with just the one card that is initially dealt—a minimum of two cards are needed for a perfect score.

Since all cards dealt out are only viewed by their individual players, an element of intrigue enters into the game. For example, if a player draws two cards and goes *over* 15, he should not give up his hand, but should try to look smug and contented in hopes that his opponent might think it will be a close game and feels pressured into taking more cards—if both players go over 15 it is a *draw*, rather than a *loss*!

✥ DRAUGHTS ✥

DRAUGHTS (pronounced "*drafts*") is a game of strategy that derived from chess around 1100 AD and has provided countless hours of entertainment for players of all ages ever since. Starting around 1774 the famous rule book, *Hoyle's Games Improved,* began to include the rules for draughts. The game is very easy to learn, yet there are several levels of strategy involved so the game actually gets more interesting and challenging the more you play it. In fact, it is claimed that consistently winning at draughts requires a higher level of strategy and skill than the much more complicated game of chess!

Draughts was precursor to the American game of "checkers," which is always played on an 8 x 8 board (eight rows of eight alternating black and white squares). The game of draughts, however, is played on a field of 10 x 10, as shown below, or sometimes even on a field of 12 x 12 squares. Today, the *official* draughts board is always 10 x 10 squares, but you can also play the game on any standard 8 x 8 square checker or chess board.

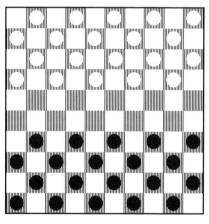

It is worth noting that no matter what color the game pieces (always called "*men*") and the squares are, the lighter shade is traditionally called "*white*" and the darker shade "*black*"—even if their colors are actually red and green! Note too that when laying out a draughts, checkers or chess board, the board should always be positioned so that a *black* square in is at the lower left corner on each player's side of the board.

The rules for draughts are basically the same as those for checkers, which just about everyone knows. In checkers the men must stay on the black squares and only advance, one square at a time, on the diagonal. The enemy's men are captured by jumping over them—so long as there is a vacant square on the opposite side of the man being captured. Once a man arrives in the last enemy row (so he can no longer advance across the board) it is "*crowned*" by placing a like-colored piece on top of it. Once crowned, a King can move back and forth and capture at will—though still on the diagonal and just one square at a time.

There are two very significant differences between the modern American game of checkers, (as just described), and Colonial-era draughts.

First of all, in draughts all of the men, whether crowned or not, can *jump backward* as well as forward! The pieces still *move* only forward, but can *capture* in any direction—so be careful as you pass an opponent's piece!

The other major difference in draughts is that once a man is crowned it can move *as many squares on a continuous diagonal as desired* (just like a bishop in chess)—both in general movement around the board and when jumping an opponent's piece. In jumping, the crowned man can also change direction *during his move*! As illustrated below, the *black* man, which has just been crowned, has jumped five of the seven remaining white men! The crowned man can either change direction or continue on the same line while jumping as long as there is an open square and none of his own men block the path (the two remaining white men are safe for the time being as the *uncrowned* black man at the upper left has blocked further jumping by the black king).

As you can see, the game of draughts can become very fast-paced once a few Kings arrive on the scene, so your best strategy is to do everything possible to prevent your opponent from being crowned and gaining this important advantage!

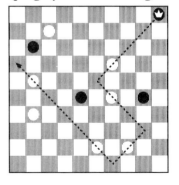

✥ TIC-TAC-TOE ✥

THIS GAME is so universally familiar as to hardly need any explanation. Tic-tac-toe game boards first appeared in Egypt around 1300 BC, and a similar game developed in China around 500 BC. The Romans brought a version of the game to England, and the distinctive game board, consisting of two pairs of intersecting lines, are often found in the ruins of Roman military campsites. This most basic of strategy games became very popular in England by around the 15th century, and it is common today among many cultures all around the world. The game can become tedious rather quickly, and so several interesting and more challenging variations are offered on the next page.

NOUGHTS AND CROSSES

The earliest specific reference to a game called "tic-tac-toe" dates from the 19th century, and this game is known by that name in America today. However, in the 18th-century it was usually called "Noughts and Crosses."

A grid of four intersecting lines are drawn out on paper, slate, piece of board or, for a quick, impromptu game, scratched out in the dirt. One player is assigned "*noughts*" (zeros or circles) and the other "*crosses*" (a simple X). The

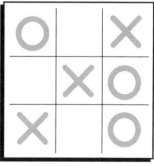

noughts *always go first*, and players take turns filling a grid space with their mark, either a nought or cross, until one player achieves three in a row (the crosses have won in the game shown here). Players switch sides after each game, so the noughts become crosses and *vice versa*.

Once players achieve proficiency at this game, the outcome is almost always a draw, and so the fun soon wears off. However, there is an ancient Roman version of this game that is played on the same board but is far more challenging!

TERNI LAPILLI (Line of Three)

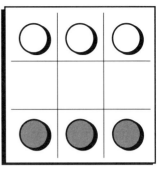

This ancient Roman game, which translates as *Three Little Stones* (and is now known as *Line of Three*) was immensely popular in its day. In addition to the usual board of four intersecting lines, you will need six markers—three each of two different colors. The pieces are arranged as shown, and players take turns moving their pieces one square at a time, in line or on the diagonal, and try to make a line of three. Players may NOT make three on their own starting "home row," but there are seven other options. This is not as easy as it might seem! There is very little space to maneuver, and you must try to block your opponent's moves and arrange your own pieces at the same time. Just one false move can lose the game!

ANOTHER FORM

This variation dates from around 1400 B.C. It was also played by the Romans and became popular in England around 1300 A.D. It is played on a board consisting of a square divided into eight, triangular sections, and can be played on the center grid of a Fox and Geese board (see page 14). Each player has three game pieces, and takes alternating turns placing a piece on any of the nine intersecting points, attempting to occupy three intersections on a given line. If no one manages to place three in a row, the players take turns moving their pieces, one intersection at a time, until one succeeds in making three in a row. Players *may not jump* another piece and must move to an adjacent, unoccupied intersection point. In the example shown here, black is about to lose as he MUST move the man at center (the others are blocked), which allows white to make three-in-a-row on the diagonal.

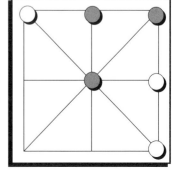

⇻ FOX AND GEESE ⇺

FOX and Geese dates from the 14th century, but is one of many descendants of an ancient strategy game called *Tafl*—which was popular in Northern Europe as early as the first century AD. There are a wide variety of games that are part of the Tafl family, but the common feature they all share is that one player is placed at a disavantage by having far fewer game pieces to work with.

Fox and Geese game boards have been found scratched out on the backs of benches and bread boards known to date from the 18th century, so the game was clearly popular during Colonial times.

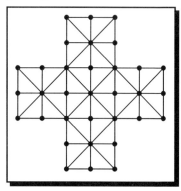

The playing board is laid out as shown here and can easily be made from a scrap of cardboard, wood, or even drawn out on a piece of paper. The players must also have a series of game pieces; *thirteen geese*, all of the same shape or color, and *one fox* of a different shape or color. The game pieces can be coins, pegs, small stones, marbles, cut-out bits of colored paper or anything else that is handy.

The object of the game is for the fox, all by himself, to move through the gaggle of geese capturing as many as possible. The geese try to immobilize the fox by getting him into a corner where he cannot move.

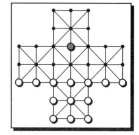

The pieces are usually arranged as shown, though the fox can actually occupy any vacant point he chooses. The fox always moves first. Both fox and geese can move along any line, forwards, backwards, diagonally or sideways (but only one space at each turn) to the next vacant point or intersection.

Only the fox can jump over his opponent so long as there is an empty point immediately behind his adversary (just like in checkers or draughts). Each captured goose is removed from the board. Several geese may be jumped by the fox in one turn, as long as there is an empty point behind each one. The fox wins if he depletes the gaggle of geese to a number that makes it impossible for them to trap him—usually less than five geese. (In the diagram, five geese have managed to corner the fox. If there were only four geese the fox would still be able to move and/or jump a goose).

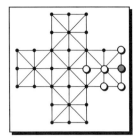

The geese cannot jump or capture the fox. They must try to gang up on him and force him into a corner so that he cannot jump or move (see above). The geese win if they succeed in immobilizing the fox. Despite the unequal numbers capturing the fox is not easy to do!

SAILOR'S SOLITAIRE

The Fox and Geese board can also be used to play a form of *solitaire*—a game played by just one player. This strategy game has been popular among sailors for several centuries, and it is said that old nails from the ship were often used for game pieces.

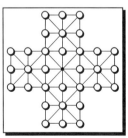

You will need 32 game pieces to fill every space on the board except for the very center. The object of the game is to jump one piece over another, always moving along only the *horizontal* or *vertical* (never diagonal) lines. When a piece is jumped it is removed from the board. See how many pieces you can jump! The ultimate goal is to remove all of the pieces from the board except the very last one. Ideally, the last remaining piece should be in the center hole!

✦ THE MILL ✦

THE MILL was also sometimes know as *Morelles* and Shakespeare refers to it as *Nine Men's Morris* in *A Midsummer's Night Dream.* The basic concept of this game is painfully simple, yet there are several levels of strategy involved so the game actually gets more interesting the more you play it! The game board is laid out as shown and can be painted onto a piece of paper, wood, cardboard or a scrap of canvas. Each player should have *nine* game pieces or *men.* These could be small stones, marbles, or bits of wood or cork, but each set of pieces should be of a different color or marked in some way so that they can be instantly distinguished from one another.

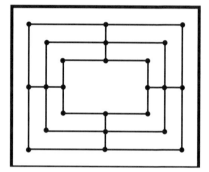

The object of the game is to place all nine of your pieces on the board and maneuver them so as to *pound* or capture your opponent's pieces. There are three phases of play in the game; *placing* the pieces, *moving* the pieces and *hopping*.

PHASE I—PLACING

In the first phase the players take turns placing one man at a time on the board. A game piece can be placed at any point where there is a corner or intersection of lines that is not already occupied by another game piece (see below right). Like in *tic-tac-toe*, each player tries to arrange three of his men in a row along any of the lines of the board. This is called forming a *mill.* If a player succeeds in forming a mill he is entitled to *pound* by removing one of his opponent's pieces from the board. A player may not, however, take away an opponent's man that is already part of a mill (unless there is no other man available). The removed game piece is then "dead" and cannot be played again.

PHASE II—MOVING

Once all of the pieces have been placed, players take turns moving their men to form new mills and further pound their opponent. A player can only move a piece in a direct line from its present position to the next vacant intersection on the board. However, players MAY form new mills by opening and then re-closing an existing mill! This is achieved by moving a man one place out of its position, and then, at the next move, returning it to it's original position. Mills may be broken and re-made any number of times, and each new mill formation entitles the player to pound his opponent.

Phase II continues until one player is reduced to having only two men remaining on the board (so that he can no longer form a mill), or until one player's pieces have been blocked so that he is unable to make a move.

PHASE III—HOPPING

Hopping is an optional phase of play that begins when either player has only three men remaining. The player is now no longer restricted to moving his men along the lines, but may "hop" to *any vacant spot* on the board to make a mill or block his opponent from making one. This sudden freedom of movement late in the game gives the losing player a clear advantage and can restore his chances of winning!

WINNING

A player is defeated when either he is reduced to only two pieces or his pieces are blocked by enemy men in such a way as to prevent any further moves.

AN EXAMPLE: During Phase I of play, black has made a horizontal mill at 1. White has blocked another black mill at 4. White has just made a vertical mill at 2, and black is poised to make a second mill by placing a man at 3. If this were Phase II, white would do well to move off of 2 and then, at his next turn, move back again (creating a fresh mill) and *pound* black at 1. Black should try to *pound* white at 2 (or the piece at the junction just above) to stop this action.

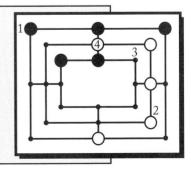

✧ SHUT THE BOX ✧

THIS IS an old game that probably originated somewhere in central Europe. By the 18th-century the game was popular among sailors and fishermen, especially in the channel islands off the coast of France. It is a wonderfully simple and addictive game that combines both an element of strategy and a bit of blind luck.

Playing shut the box involves the construction of a special game box, though it can also be played without (see below). This box measures about seven by ten inches and is about two inches deep. The upper third of the box is framed up into a shallow shelf, which is divided into nine narrow compartments. The upper half of each of these compartments bears a number from *one* to *nine*, and a small sliding door is fitted over each so that the number can be covered and uncovered as needed. It may sound complicated, but there is really very little skill required to build the game box and the accompanying diagram should prove sufficient in guiding you through construction (below).

At the beginning of play, all of the doors are *opened* so that all nine numbers are exposed. The first player then rolls a *pair of dice*, and either adds up the *total* or plays *each die separately* and closes up the door or doors of the corresponding number or numbers.

For example, if a *five* and a *four* are rolled, the player can

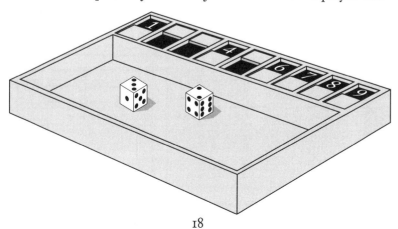

18

cover either the *five* and the *four* or the *nine*. If a *two* and a *six* are rolled, the player can cover either the *two* and the *six* or the *eight*.

The same player continues to roll the dice and cover the corresponding numbers until a combination is rolled that cannot be played. In the illustration shown, a *three* and a *two* have been rolled, but the *two*, *three* and *five* (the only numbers applicable) have already been covered, and so the player's turn is over. The *remaining numbers* still exposed are then added up and the dice passed to the next player.

Note that the number *one* cannot possibly be rolled with two dice and so once the *sum of the exposed numbers* totals *six or less*, one die is discarded and the player continues to roll with just a single die.

Players take turns rolling the dice, covering the corresponding numbers and adding up the points still exposed until one player's cumulative score totals 45— at which point he *loses*! The remaining players continue on, and as the points of each player total 45 they too are out of the game. *The last player left is the winner.* Obviously the object is for a player to cover as many numbers as he can during his turn to keep his score as low as possible for as long as possible.

The shut the box game board is an entertaining little gadget that can be made as plain or as fancy as desired. However, the device is not entirely necessary for playing this game. A game board can be crafted from a piece of wood, scrap of fabric or even an ordinary sheet of paper by dividing it into nine equal squares—like the common tic-tac-toe grid. Each square is assigned a number, as indicated above, and game tokens, small bits of paper, stones or coins can be used to cover each number as it is played.

9	8	7
6	5	4
3	2	1

⋙ DICE GAMES ⋘

ULTI-SIDED gaming pieces with various designs or figures inscribed on each surface have been found at sites dating from ancient England, Greece and the Roman empire. Similar pieces have also been found at Mayan sites in Central America. Though the original use for many of these game pieces is lost to us, the first recorded game of chance using dice is the Egyptian game *astragali*, which dates to 3500 B.C.

Your dice must be perfectly alike in size and shape, with all sides square. Each *die* face is marked with a series of *pips* as shown, placed so that the

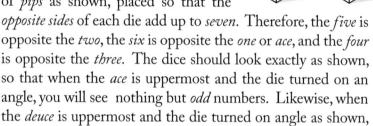

opposite sides of each die add up to *seven*. Therefore, the *five* is opposite the *two*, the *six* is opposite the *one* or *ace*, and the *four* is opposite the *three*. The dice should look exactly as shown, so that when the *ace* is uppermost and the die turned on an angle, you will see nothing but *odd* numbers. Likewise, when the *deuce* is uppermost and the die turned on angle as shown, you should see all *even* numbers.

Although they can be thrown from the hand, dice were almost always thrown from a dice box in the 18th century. These were often made of turned wood, but could also be made from leather or *papier maché*.

You can easily make your own *papier maché* dice box from the cardboard core of a toilet paper roll. Cut the tube to a length of 2½" or 3" and carefully trace the outside diameter onto a scrap of this cardboard (like the back of a legal pad), and cut out the disk. Then, tear up a sheet of old newspaper into narrow strips between ½" and 1" wide and six or seven inches long. Put some warm water into a shallow bowl and sprinkle flour into it, stirring the mixture until it is smooth and free of lumps. Add flour a little at a time and stir until you create a paste about as thick as heavy cream.

Now, drag your paper strips through the paste mixture

and use them to tape the cardboard disk to the bottom of your tube. Smooth out any wrinkles as much as you can, then set the box aside to dry for several hours. Once the bottom has set up, you may resume applying newspaper strips, carefully covering every surface, inside and out. Let it dry over night then paint your dice box a dark color.

Now you are ready to throw dice!

HAZARD

The game of *Hazard* is an early version of the modern casino game of "craps." The game's origins date back several centuries and it is even mentioned in William Shakespeare's *Henry the IV*. Edmond Hoyle's 1779 rules for Hazard include some very detailed score-keeping and odds tables that were designed to make the game more challenging. I think those early rules are unnecessarily complicated, therefore a more simplified version is presented here.

Hazard uses a pair of dice and is played by two or more players. It is usually a betting game, but can also be played simply for fun. To start, each player throws a single die and the highest point takes up the dice. This player then throws or *casts* the dice until he loses, with the object being to retain possession of the dice for as long as possible.

When a pair of dice are thrown and the total pips tallied there are eleven possible scores that may result. If the roll is a *seven* or *eleven*, the caster *wins* instantly. If the throw is a *two, three* or *twelve*, the caster *loses*. If the roll is a *four, five, six, eight, nine* or *ten*, then the caster continues to throw until he either throws the *same number again*, or he throws a *seven*. If he throws the same number, he *wins*. If he throws a seven before rolling the same number, he *loses* and passes the dice to the next player. Any throws besides a seven or the same number do not count and the caster continues to throw.

Note that the throw simply has to add up to the same number, not necessarily show exactly the same pattern of pips. For example, if the caster throws *two fours* (an eight), he can still win by throwing a *three* and a *five* or a *two* and a *six*.

GOING TO BOSTON

This is another simple little game that is said to have originated in the 18th century. It was also known as "*Yankee Grab*" or "*Newmarket.*" The game uses *three* dice and can be played by two or more players.

The first player rolls all three dice, and sets the highest number aside. He then rolls the remaining two dice. Again, he sets the highest number aside, and rolls the remaining die. The total of the three dice is added up, and the player passes the dice to the other player (if more than two play, the dice are passed to the left). Play continues in this fashion, the winner being the first one to reach a total score of 100 points.

There are also two ways to throw "bonus" scores. If the player casts *three-of-a-kind* on his first throw, it scores 30 points no matter what the combination is. If he casts *two-of-a-kind* with his second throw, it scores 15 points regardless of the face value. In both cases, the player sets aside one die, casts out the remainder of his turn and adds up the score as usual.

INN AND INN

Inn and Inn is a simple gambling game from Charles Cotton's *Compleat Gamester,* which was published in 1674. It is played by either two or three players using some sort of gaming tokens like pennies or hard candies. The *stake* (the number of tokens for each drop), and the *battle* (maximum number of tokens each person will play) should be determined before play commences. The game is over for a player when all of his pennies or tokens are gone.

Each player should have his own dice box, equipped with four dice, and players take turns casting all four dice. If a player throws *doublets* (two-of-a-kind), he is *Inn*, and must surrender a stake (one or more gaming tokens) to the pot. If the player throws either *two pair* or *four-of-a-kind*, then he is *Inn and Inn* and wins the entire pot.

If the player throws neither an *Inn* nor an *Inn and Inn*, his adversary wins the pot or, if playing with three, the two remaining adversaries may either split the pot, or continue to throw to see if one of them can win it all!

✤ DOMINOES ✤

OMINOES is a very simple strategic matching game. In the late 18th century the game pieces were usually made of bone and lost dominoes have been found at several colonial-era archeological sites.

Dominoes are arranged in suits similar to playing cards. Each domino consists of two halves, and each half holds a series of dots or *pips* representing the numbers zero through six (see below). Because it has two halves, each domino belongs to two different *suits*. The Six Suit is shown below, but note that the lower number on each domino shows the other suit to which it belongs. For example, the center domino below belongs to both the *six* and the *three* suits.

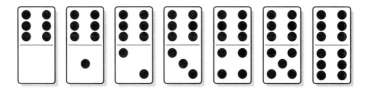

DOMINOES

In the basic game, two to four players take turns laying down their dominoes by *matching* the pips.

First, all 28 dominoes are laid face down on a flat surface and are shuffled by both players by scooting them around in a random fashion. Next, each player draws *seven* dominoes, taking turns pulling them out of the central pile, which is traditionally called the *bone yard*.

The players examine their dominoes and arrange them either in their hands or on the table, being careful to conceal the pips from the other players. To help avoid confusion it is usually best for each player to arrange their dominoes in suits by seniority, placing the dominos with the most pips on the left and with the least pips on the right.

The player with the *highest double* sets first. For example, if no player has drawn the double six, then the double five or the double four is played first.

The other player then lays one of his dominoes, one end of which must match the double that was laid. For example, in the illustration below, the *double six* was set, and the opponent laid the *six/one* to the left. Then, taking alternating turns, the six/three, three/four, four/two and double two were laid. Note that a bend can be put into the layout whenever it is convenient, but that doubles are *always* placed perpendicular to the current path. The next domino can be played at either end of the layout (off of the six/one or off of the double two), but if played off of the double two it must be played from the center and not one of the ends.

When a player does not have a domino in his hand that matches one or the other end of the layout, he must draw additional dominoes or *bones* from the bone yard until he finds one that can be played. If all of the bones are gone, then he must pass his turn to his opponent. The game is won by the first player to succeed in placing all of his dominoes in the layout.

Though a simple enough game to master, some strategy is needed in placing your dominoes if you hope to win consistently. Try to plan a few moves ahead and lay your bones so that you can play your next domino at either end of the layout. That way, if your opponent places his piece at one end of the layout and you do not have a bone that matches, you can still play to the other end! This is not as simple as it sounds, but with some concentration and by keeping track of which dominoes have already been played you will be able to anticipate your opponent's moves and plan your dominoes accordingly.

MUGGINS

Muggins is a variation on the standard domino game. It is an old traditional pub game and is also sometimes known as *Five Up*. It is thought to have originated in France toward the end of the 18th century and been brought to America through New Orleans. By the middle of the 19th century muggins was a very popular game in the American west.

Muggins is for two to four players, and four players can also play as two teams of two. The object is to accumulate as many points as possible, as the player(s) with the *most points* at the end of the game *wins*.

The game starts out exactly like regular dominoes, only the first player can play any domino he chooses—it does not need to be a double. What makes muggins unique is the manner in which it is scored, which is quite simple; a player scores points whenever the *sum of the two open ends* of the layout totals a multiple of *five*. For example, if the player places a bone whose open end is *four*, and the other end of the layout has an open *one*, that player scores *five points*. If the next player places a bone to match the *one* so that the open ends of the layout are now a *four* and a *six*, that player scores *ten points*. Doubles are placed perpendicular to the path as in regular dominoes, but they only count for the face value of the suit. For example, in the illustration on the opposite page, the sum of the two dominoes that form the open ends of the layout counts as *three*, not *five*.

If a player should play a tile and overlook the score, any opponent may call "muggins!" and claim the score for himself (after allowing a reasonable amount of time for the original player to claim the score).

Play continues either until someone plays his last bone, or until all players can no longer match any dominoes and have consecutively passed. The player who finishes first or, if everyone has passed, the player with the *least total number* of pips on his remaining bones wins. The winner also gets to add the total number of pips on the remaining bones in the hands of *all other players* to his score.

✦ BIBLIOGRAPHY ✦

Bell, R. C., *The Board Game Book* (Los Angeles: The Knapp Press, 1979)

Benham, W. Gurney, *Playing Cards* (London: Spring Books, 1953)

Boswell's London Journal, 1762-1763, Frederick A. Pottle, editor (New York: McGraw-Hill, 1950)

Boswell, James, *The Life of Samuel Johnson, with Marginal Comments by Mrs. Piozzi*, three volumes, Edward G. Fletcher, editor (New York: The Heritage Press, 1963)

Boswell, James, *A Tour to the Outer Hebrides with Samuel Johnson, L.L.D.*, Frederick A. Pottle, editor (New York: The Literary Guild, Inc., 1936)

Cotton, Charles, *The Compleat Gamester*, (Barre, MA: Imprint Society, 1970) [originally published 1674]

Curwen, Samuel, *The Journal of Samuel Curwen, Loyalist*, two volumes, Andrew Oliver, editor (Cambridge: Harvard University Press, 1972)

Encyclopædia Britannica, or, a Dictionary of the Arts and Sciences, three volumes (Edinburgh: Bell & MacFarquhar, 1771) [Facsimile edition, ca. 1970]

The Gentleman's Magazine, (London: Sylvanus Urban [Edward Cave, David Henry, *et al*], 1740-1804)

Hawkins, Christopher, *The Adventures of Christopher Hawkins*, (New York: New York Times & Arno Press, 1968)

Hoyle's Games Improved, Being Practical Treatises on the following Fashionable Games... Charles Jones, editor (London: J. F. Rivington, 1779)

Hoyle's Games Improved, Containing the Established Rules and Practice of... (Philadelphia: Henry F. Anners, 1845)

Hoyle's Complete and Authoritative Book of Games (Garden City, New York: Blue Ribbon Books, 1940)

Hume, Ivor Noël, *A Guide to Artifacts of Colonial America* (New York: Alfred Knopf, 1970)

Johnson, Dr. Samuel, *A Dictionary of the English Language* (London: 1755) [facsimile edition, Times Books, 1979]

Neumann, George C. and Kravic, Frank J., *Collector's Illustrated Encyclopedia of the American Revolution*, (Harrisburg, Pennsylvania: Stackpole Books, 1975)

The Diary of Samuel Pepys, 1659-1669, two volumes, Henry Wheatley, F. S. A., editor (New York: Heritage Press, 1942)

Tilley, Roger, *A History of Playing Cards* (New York: Clarkson N. Potter, 1973)

The Diary of Thomas Turner, 1754-1765, David Vaisey, editor (Oxford: Oxford University Press, 1985)

The Yale Shakespeare, The Complete Works, Wilbur L. Cross and Tucker Brooke, editors (New York: Barnes & Noble, 1993)